INTRODUCTION: UNDERSTANDING THE AI AROUND US

Something big is happening in our world, and it's affecting all of us. The largest companies in America – names you know like Google, Apple, and Microsoft – are using artificial intelligence (AI) systems that have become incredibly powerful. These systems are so advanced that they're changing how we live, work, and make decisions, often in ways we don't even notice.

Think about your day so far. Maybe you asked Siri or Alexa about the weather. Perhaps you used Google Maps to avoid traffic on your way to work. You might have gotten recommendations for what to watch on Netflix or what to buy on Amazon. These are all examples of AI working in your life. But here's what many people don't realize: these everyday examples are just the tip of the iceberg.

Behind the scenes, much more powerful AI systems are making decisions that affect your life in bigger ways. They might help decide whether you get a job interview, what interest rate you're offered on a loan, or what news and information you see online.

Some experts believe these systems are becoming so advanced that they might be approaching – or even exceeding – human-level intelligence in certain areas.

Why This Book Matters

This book exists because you deserve to understand what's happening with AI, even if you're not a technology expert. You don't need to know computer programming or advanced math to understand how AI affects your life and how to protect yourself and your family.

We wrote this book in clear, everyday language because this information is too important to be locked away in technical jargon. Whether you're comfortable with technology or find it overwhelming, this book will help you:

- Understand what AI really is and how it works in your daily life
- Protect yourself and your family from AI-related risks
- Make smart decisions about using AI tools
- Know your rights when dealing with AI systems
- Take action when you need to

How to Use This Book

Each chapter builds on the one before it, but you can also jump to the sections that interest you most. We've included real examples, practical tips, and clear explanations throughout. The Quick Reference Guide at the end gives you important information you might need in a hurry.

We've organized the book to answer the questions most people have about AI:

- What is it actually doing in my life right now?
- How can I use it safely?
- What should I watch out for?
- How do I protect my privacy?
- What do I do if something goes wrong?

A Note About Language

You'll notice we've kept our language simple and clear. That's not because we think you can't handle complex ideas – it's because AI is complicated enough without adding fancy words to the mix. Even experts sometimes struggle to explain AI in simple terms. We believe that understanding AI shouldn't require a college degree.

Looking Ahead

The world of AI is changing quickly, but the basic principles you'll learn in this book will help you understand and deal with these changes. We'll start with the basics and build up to more complex ideas, always focusing on what matters most to your daily life.

Remember: You don't need to become an AI expert. You just need to understand enough to make good decisions and protect yourself in this changing world. That's exactly what this book will help you do.

Let's begin by looking at what's really happening with AI in the biggest companies in America, and what it means for all of us.

[Next Chapter: Understanding the Basics]

PART 1: UNDERSTANDING THE BASICS

What's Really Happening with AI

Something big is happening in the world of technology, and it's changing faster than most people realize. The computers and programs that big companies use today aren't just following simple instructions anymore – they're learning, making decisions, and becoming incredibly smart in ways that affect every part of your life.

Think about the last time you used your smartphone. Maybe you asked it for directions, and it warned you about traffic ahead. Or perhaps you took a photo, and it automatically made the colors look better. These might seem like simple things, but they're examples of artificial intelligence working to help you.

But here's what's really important to understand: The AI we see in our everyday lives is just the tip of the iceberg. Big companies like Google, Apple, and Microsoft are developing AI systems that are much more powerful than what we usually see. These advanced systems can learn from billions of pieces of information, make decisions faster than any human, and handle many complex tasks at once.

Some experts believe these systems are becoming so advanced that they might be getting close to thinking like humans do – or maybe even better than humans in some ways. This is why we call them "Silicon Gods." They're becoming so powerful that they're changing how our world works, often in ways we don't even notice.

Simple Explanations of Key Terms

When people talk about AI, they often use technical words that can be confusing. Let's break down what these terms really mean in everyday language.

When you hear about "**Narrow AI**," that's what we use every day. It's AI that's really good at one specific job, like recognizing faces in photos or giving you directions. Think of it like a skilled worker who's an expert at one thing but can't do much else.

"**Artificial General Intelligence**" (AGI) is different – it's what companies are trying to create now. This would be AI that can think about any problem, just like a human can. Imagine a helper that could understand and do any task you explain to them, just like a person would.

Then there's "**Artificial Super Intelligence**" (ASI), which would be AI that's smarter than humans at almost everything. Some people think the biggest tech companies might be getting close to creating this, or possibly even being run by it, which is both exciting and scary.

You'll also hear about "**machine learning**" – that's just the way AI gets better at its job by looking at lots of examples, kind of like how you get better at something by practicing. And when people talk about "algorithms," they're just talking about the steps the AI follows to do its job, like a recipe for cooking.

The Companies Leading the AI Revolution

The biggest tech companies are racing to develop more powerful AI systems, and you're probably using their technology every day without realizing it.

Google is like the librarian of the internet, but with AI, it's become more like a smart friend who can help you find anything and understand it. When you search for something, Google's AI doesn't just find words that match – it tries to understand what you're really asking for and gives you the best answer, even if you don't use the exact right words.

Microsoft is changing how we work and play with AI. If you've used newer versions of Word or PowerPoint, you might have noticed they can suggest better ways to write or design your work. Through their partnership with OpenAI, they're also behind ChatGPT, which can have amazingly human-like conversations.

Apple takes a different approach, focusing on making AI work while protecting your privacy. When you use Siri or take photos on an iPhone, the AI works right on your device instead of sending your information to the internet. This means you get the benefits of AI while keeping your personal information more private.

Amazon uses AI to transform shopping and how the internet works. Not only does it predict what you might want to buy, but through its Amazon Web Services (AWS), it also provides AI tools that power many other websites and apps you use every day.

Meta (the company that owns Facebook and Instagram) uses AI to decide what you see when you scroll through social media.

Their AI learns what kinds of posts keep you interested and shows you more of those, while also working to spot and remove fake accounts and harmful content.

How We Got Here: The Story of AI in Plain English

The story of how we got to today's powerful AI systems is fascinating and important to understand. It didn't happen overnight – it's been a journey of over 70 years.

In the 1950s, scientists first started wondering if computers could think like humans. Back then, computers were huge machines that could barely do simple math. Most people thought the idea of smart machines was just science fiction.

Through the 1980s and 1990s, computers got better at specific tasks. They could play chess and do complicated calculations, but they still weren't very good at things that humans find easy, like recognizing faces or understanding speech.

The real breakthrough came in the 2000s when the internet gave AI systems access to huge amounts of information to learn from. Imagine trying to learn a new language – it's much easier if you have lots of examples to study. That's what the internet provided for AI.

In the 2010s, companies started investing billions of dollars in

AI development. Computers got powerful enough to process massive amounts of information quickly, and AI got much better at understanding pictures, words, and even human speech.

Now, in the 2020s, we're seeing AI that can have real conversations, create art, write stories, and make decisions that affect many parts of our lives. Some systems are becoming so advanced that they're raising big questions about the future: What happens when machines can think as well as humans? Who controls these systems? How do we make sure they help rather than harm us?

Understanding these basics helps you make sense of how AI is changing our world and what it means for you personally. In the next chapters, we'll look at how AI affects your daily life and what you can do to make it work better for you while protecting yourself and your family.

[Next: We'll explore how AI is already part of your everyday life and what that means for you.]

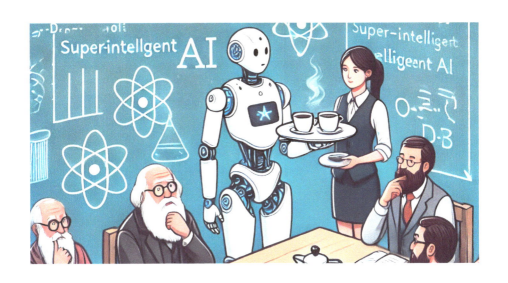

PART 2: AI IN YOUR DAILY LIFE

Your Phone, Apps, and AI

E very time you pick up your phone, you're holding a device packed with artificial intelligence. Let's talk about how AI is working behind the scenes all day long.

When you wake up and check your weather app, AI has already analyzed weather patterns and adjusted the forecast just for your location. As you type a text message to your friend, AI is correcting your spelling and suggesting the next word you might want to use. Even when you take a morning selfie, AI is working to make sure your photo looks good by adjusting the lighting and focusing on your face.

Your phone's AI assistant (like Siri or Google Assistant) does more than just answer questions. It learns your daily routine, remembers your preferences, and tries to be helpful at just the right moments. When you're running late for work, it might automatically suggest a faster route. When you're playing music, it learns what songs you like and creates playlists just for you.

But there's something important to know: your phone's AI is always learning from how you use it. This helps make your experience better, but it also means the phone knows a lot about your habits. In the privacy section later, we'll talk about how to control what information you share.

Shopping and AI: What You Need to Know

Shopping has changed dramatically because of AI, whether you're buying online or in a store. Let's look at how AI affects your shopping experience and your wallet.

When you shop online, AI acts like a very attentive personal shopper. It remembers what you've bought before, what you've looked at, and even how long you spent looking at different items. This is why you might see ads for running shoes right after you've been browsing exercise equipment. The AI is trying to predict what you might want to buy next.

In physical stores, AI is working too, even if you can't see it. Many stores use AI to decide what products to stock, where to put them on shelves, and when to offer sales. Those loyalty cards that give you special discounts? They're powered by AI that studies your shopping patterns to offer deals it thinks you'll like.

Here's something most people don't know: AI often helps set prices. These prices can change throughout the day based on many factors, including how many people are shopping, what's in stock, and what competitors are charging. This is why that item you've been watching might suddenly go on sale – or become more expensive.

Social Media: How AI Shows You Content

Social media might feel random, but it's actually carefully controlled by AI. Understanding how this works can help you better control what you see and share.

Every time you open a social media app, AI is making thousands of quick decisions about what to show you. It looks at posts you've liked before, how long you spend reading certain types of content, and even what your friends are interested in. This is why no two people's social media feeds look exactly the same.

The AI remembers everything you do on these platforms: every like, share, comment, and how long you pause while scrolling. It uses this information to create a detailed picture of what it thinks will keep you interested and engaged. Sometimes this means showing you things you agree with, and sometimes it means showing you things that might make you feel strong emotions.

What's important to understand is that social media AI is designed to keep you using the app as long as possible. This means it might not always show you the most important or useful content, but rather what it thinks will keep you scrolling. Being aware of this can help you make better choices about how you spend your time online.

Banking and AI: Protecting Your Money

AI has become your invisible financial guardian, working around the clock to protect your money and help you manage it better. This is one area where AI's constant monitoring can really work in your favor.

When you use your credit card, AI checks each purchase in real time. It knows your usual spending patterns so well that it can spot potentially fraudulent charges instantly. That's why you might get a text asking if you really meant to buy something when you're traveling or making an unusual purchase. This automatic fraud detection stops millions of dollars in theft every day.

Modern banking apps use AI to help you manage your money better. They can predict your upcoming bills, warn you if you might overdraw your account, and even suggest ways to save money based on your spending habits. Some banks' AI can look at your regular expenses and tell you if you're paying more than average for things like utilities or phone services.

The AI in banking is also getting better at helping people get loans and credit cards. Instead of just looking at your credit score, many banks now use AI to consider many different factors about how you handle money. This can sometimes help people get approved even if they don't have a perfect credit history.

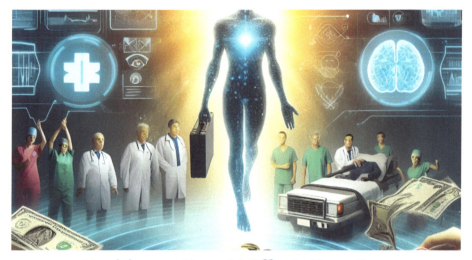

Healthcare: How AI Affects Your Care

AI is changing healthcare in ways that affect the care you receive, often without you knowing it. Let's explore how AI is working to help keep you healthy.

When you visit your doctor, AI might be helping them make better decisions about your care. It can analyze your symptoms, medical history, and test results much faster than any human could. This doesn't replace your doctor's judgment, but it gives them more information to work with when deciding how to help you.

If you've ever had an X-ray or MRI, AI probably helped analyze it. These systems can spot potential problems that might be hard for human eyes to see. They can also compare your results with millions of other images to help doctors make more accurate diagnoses.

AI is also working behind the scenes at your pharmacy. It helps make sure your prescriptions are safe by checking for possible drug interactions and alerting pharmacists to potential problems. It can even help predict when you'll need a refill and have it ready before you ask.

For people with chronic conditions, AI-powered devices can be especially helpful. Smart watches can detect irregular heartbeats, predict asthma attacks before they happen, and even alert emergency services if you fall. These devices learn your normal patterns and can spot when something isn't right.

Remember that while AI is becoming an important part of healthcare, it's still just a tool to help your healthcare providers make better decisions. The human judgment of trained medical professionals remains essential for your care.

[Next chapter: We'll look at how AI is changing workplaces and what this means for your job.]

PART 3: AI AT WORK

How AI is Changing Different Jobs

T he way we work is changing because of AI, and it's happening faster than many people realize. Whether you work in an office, a store, a factory, or from home, AI is probably already affecting your job in some way. Let's talk about what this means for you.

If you work in an office, you might notice that computers are getting better at doing some of the repetitive parts of your job. AI can now write simple reports, answer basic customer emails, and even schedule meetings for you. But here's something important to understand: AI isn't usually replacing entire jobs. Instead, it's changing how we do our work, often by handling the boring tasks so we can focus on more important things.

For people who work in stores or restaurants, AI helps predict how busy you'll be and what customers might want to buy. It can tell managers how many workers they'll need each day and what products to keep in stock. Some stores now use AI to help customers find items or answer questions, but they still need human workers to help with more complicated problems and provide personal service.

In factories and warehouses, AI works with robots to move and package items. But it's not just about replacing human workers – AI also helps make jobs safer by spotting potential dangers before accidents happen. It can tell when machines need fixing and help workers do their jobs better.

Healthcare workers are seeing big changes too. AI helps doctors spot problems in X-rays and suggests possible treatments, but it doesn't make the final decisions. Nurses and medical staff use AI to keep track of patients and catch potential problems early. The AI is like a helpful assistant, not a replacement for trained medical professionals.

Keeping Your Job Skills Updated

With all these changes happening, you might wonder how to keep your job skills current. The good news is that you don't need to become a computer programmer or AI expert to stay valuable at work.

The most important skills for working with AI are often things humans are naturally good at: solving unexpected problems, being creative, working well with other people, and making judgment calls when things aren't clear. These are skills that AI still struggles with, and they're becoming more valuable, not less.

Many companies now offer free training to help their workers learn to use AI tools. Take advantage of these opportunities when you can. Even learning basic things about how AI works can help you feel more confident about using new tools at work.

It's also good to learn about AI tools that are specific to your type of work. For example, if you work in customer service, learning how to work with AI chatbots can make your job easier. If you work in an office, knowing how to use AI writing and analysis tools can help you work faster and better.

Working Alongside AI Systems

Working with AI is becoming a normal part of many jobs, so let's talk about how to do it well. Think of AI as a tool, like a very smart calculator or a helpful assistant. It can do some things incredibly well, but it needs human oversight to make sure everything is done right.

When you're working with AI, it's important to double-check its work, especially for important tasks. AI can make mistakes or misunderstand things, just like people can. Your experience and judgment are crucial for catching these mistakes and making sure everything makes sense.

Some people worry that AI will take over their job, but understanding how to work with AI often makes you more valuable to your employer. It's like learning to use any new tool – the people who know how to use it well become more important, not less.

New Job Opportunities with AI

While some jobs are changing because of AI, new jobs are also being created. Many of these new jobs don't require advanced technical skills – they need people who can help bridge the gap between AI systems and regular workers or customers.

For example, companies need people who can:

- Explain AI tools to other workers
- Check AI work for mistakes or problems
- Help customers use AI-powered services
- Give feedback about how AI systems are working

- Train AI systems with real-world examples

These jobs often rely more on people skills than technical knowledge. If you're good at explaining things, solving problems, or helping others learn new skills, you might be perfect for one of these new roles.

Protecting Yourself from Job Changes

While AI brings opportunities, it's smart to protect yourself from unwanted changes in your work. Here are some practical ways to do that:

First, pay attention to how AI is being used in your industry. Read industry news, talk to coworkers, and notice when new tools are introduced at work. This helps you see changes coming before they affect your job.

Second, focus on building skills that AI can't easily copy. These include building relationships with customers or coworkers, solving unexpected problems, and making complex decisions that require understanding human needs and feelings.

Third, try to learn about new AI tools before you have to use them at work. Many online courses and tutorials can help you understand these tools, and many are free or low-cost.

Finally, keep records of how you use AI to make your work better. This shows your value to your employer and can help you find new opportunities if you need them.

Looking Ahead

The future of work with AI might seem uncertain, but remember this: throughout history, new technologies have always changed how we work. Just like people adapted to computers and smartphones, we can adapt to AI. The key is to stay informed, keep learning, and focus on the human skills that make you valuable.

In the next chapter, we'll look at how to protect yourself and your family while using AI systems in your daily life. We'll talk about privacy, security, and making smart choices about when and how to use AI tools.

[Next: Part 4 - Protecting Yourself and Your Family in an AI World]

PART 4: PROTECTING YOURSELF AND YOUR FAMILY

Privacy Tips Anyone Can Use

L iving with AI doesn't mean you have to give up your privacy. Think of privacy like the curtains in your house – you get to decide when to open them and when to keep them closed. Let's talk about simple ways to protect your personal information while still using helpful AI tools.

Start with your phone, since it's probably the device you use most. Every time you download a new app, it usually asks for permission to access different things – your location, your contacts, your photos. You don't have to say yes to everything. Think about whether the app really needs that information to work. Does a calculator app really need to know where you are? Does a game really need access to your contacts?

On social media, AI systems are always watching what you like, share, and comment on. They use this information to show you more content and ads. Take a few minutes to check your privacy settings on each social media account. You can usually limit who sees your posts and what information the platform can collect about you.

When you use smart speakers or AI assistants at home, remember that they're always listening for their wake word ("Hey Siri" or "Alexa"). Most of these devices have a mute button or switch. It's smart to use it when you're having private conversations. You can also go into the device's settings and delete your voice recordings regularly.

Keeping Your Kids Safe Online

Protecting children in a world of AI requires special attention, but it doesn't have to be overwhelming. The goal is to help kids enjoy the benefits of technology while staying safe from its risks.

Start by talking with your kids about AI in ways they can understand. Explain that when they're online, they're often interacting with computers that try to figure out what they like and what they might want to see next. Help them understand that not everything they see online is real or true, and that AI systems might show them things just to keep them watching or playing longer.

For younger children, use parental controls on devices and apps. These tools have gotten much better at spotting potential problems. They can block inappropriate content, limit screen time, and alert you if something seems wrong. But remember – these controls aren't perfect, and they're not a replacement for talking with your kids about online safety.

Teach your children about privacy in simple terms. Tell them not to share personal information online, like their full name, address, or school. Help them understand that pictures and videos they share might stay online forever, even if they delete them later.

Spotting AI-Created Scams

Scammers are using AI to make their tricks more convincing, but there are ways to spot and avoid them. The key is knowing what to look for and trusting your instincts when something doesn't feel right.

AI can now create fake photos, videos, and even voice recordings that look and sound real. If you get a phone call that sounds like a family member asking for money, or a video that shows something that seems unbelievable, be skeptical. Scammers can use AI to copy someone's voice or create fake emergency situations.

Watch out for AI-written emails and messages that try to trick you into sharing personal information or sending money. These messages are getting better at sounding natural and personal. If you get an unexpected message asking you to act quickly or keep something secret, that's usually a warning sign.

Remember this rule: legitimate businesses and government agencies won't ask for sensitive information through email, text, or phone calls. If someone contacts you asking for passwords, banking information, or social security numbers, it's probably a scam – even if the message looks official.

Managing Your Digital Life

Taking control of your digital life means understanding how AI systems use your information and making conscious choices about what you share. Think of it like organizing your house – you want to keep the useful things while getting rid of what you don't need.

Start by doing a "digital cleanup." Go through your online accounts and delete ones you don't use anymore. Check the privacy settings on the accounts you keep. Look at what apps are installed on your devices and remove any you haven't used in the last few months.

Create strong passwords for your accounts, and don't use the same password everywhere. Password manager apps can help you create and remember complex passwords. They're much safer than using simple passwords or the same password for everything.

Be thoughtful about what you share on social media. AI systems can learn a lot about you from your posts, photos, and likes. They can figure out your habits, interests, and even predict your future behavior. Share only what you're comfortable with the world knowing.

Making Smart Choices with AI Tools

AI tools can be incredibly helpful, but it's important to use them wisely. Think of AI like a powerful car – it can take you where you want to go, but you need to stay in control and follow the safety rules.

When you're using AI tools for important tasks, like writing work emails or making financial decisions, always review the results carefully. AI can make mistakes or suggest things that aren't quite right for your situation. Trust your judgment – if something doesn't look right, double-check it or ask for human help.

Be careful about what personal information you share with AI systems. Even if a service seems private, assume that anything you tell an AI might be stored and analyzed. Don't share sensitive information like passwords, financial details, or private family matters unless you're using a secure, trusted service.

Remember that AI systems are designed to keep you engaged and sometimes to influence your choices. When you're shopping online or using social media, take breaks to think about whether you're making decisions because you want to, or because AI is nudging you in that direction.

Looking Forward

As AI becomes more advanced, new privacy and security challenges will appear. But by understanding the basics of how AI works and following simple safety practices, you can protect yourself and your family while still enjoying the benefits of these technologies.

In the next chapter, we'll explore the bigger questions about AI's role in society and what it means for our future. We'll look at how to stay informed about AI developments and make your voice heard in decisions about how AI is used.

[Next: Part 5 - Big Questions Made Simple]

PART 6: TAKING ACTION

Making Your Voice Heard

You might think that ordinary people can't influence how AI develops, but that's not true. Your voice matters, and there are many ways to make it heard. Let's talk about how you can help shape the future of AI in your community and beyond.

Start with the companies you use every day. When you notice problems with AI systems – like biased recommendations or privacy concerns – report them. Most big tech companies have feedback forms or customer service channels. They pay attention when many people raise the same concerns. Your feedback helps them improve their systems and understand what matters to their users.

You can also influence how AI is used in your workplace. If your company is introducing new AI tools, share your thoughts about what works and what doesn't. Your practical experience with these systems is valuable information for decision-makers. Don't be afraid to speak up about problems or suggest improvements.

Local government meetings are another place where your voice matters. Many cities and towns are deciding how to use AI in public services, from traffic control to emergency response. These meetings are open to the public, and officials often want to hear from regular people about their concerns and ideas.

Protecting Your Rights

You have rights when it comes to AI systems, but you need to know what they are and how to defend them. Think of this like knowing your rights as a consumer – the more you know, the better you can protect yourself.

First, you have the right to know when AI is being used to make important decisions about your life. This includes job applications, loan applications, and insurance decisions. If you think an AI system made an unfair decision about you, you can usually request an explanation and challenge the decision.

You also have privacy rights. In many places, companies must tell you what information they collect about you and how they use it. They need your permission to share your information with others. You can usually request to see what information companies have about you and ask them to delete it.

When you're signing up for new services or downloading apps, take time to read the privacy policies – or at least the main points. Look for information about how your data will be used and what choices you have. Don't be afraid to say no to services that want more information than they need.

Teaching Your Family About AI

One of the most important things you can do is help your family understand and use AI safely. You don't need to be a tech expert to do this – you just need to share what you've learned and encourage smart habits.

Talk with your family about how AI affects your daily lives. Point out examples of AI in action, like when social media suggests friends or when streaming services recommend shows. Help them understand that these suggestions come from computers analyzing their behavior.

Make AI safety a regular topic of family discussion. Share tips about protecting personal information, spotting fake content, and using AI tools responsibly. Encourage questions and admit when you don't know something – learning about AI is an ongoing process for everyone.

Set family guidelines for using AI-powered devices and services. This might include rules about sharing personal information, using social media, or when to turn off smart devices. Make sure everyone understands why these guidelines matter.

Getting Involved in AI Decisions

You can take an active role in how AI is developed and used in your community. There are more opportunities to get involved than you might think.

Join local technology groups or community organizations that discuss AI issues. Many libraries and community centers host workshops or discussion groups about technology. These are great places to learn more and connect with others who share your concerns.

Pay attention to proposed laws and regulations about AI. When governments ask for public comments on new rules, share your thoughts. Your real-world experiences with AI can help shape better policies.

Consider joining or supporting organizations that work for responsible AI development. Many groups focus on making sure AI benefits everyone, not just big companies. You can help by volunteering, sharing information, or supporting their work in other ways.

Planning for the Future

The world of AI will keep changing, but you can prepare yourself and your family for these changes. Think of it like preparing for any other big change in life – the better prepared you are, the more confidently you can handle what comes.

Stay informed about AI developments, but don't feel overwhelmed by trying to understand everything. Focus on changes that might affect your life, work, or family directly. Look for reliable sources of information that explain things clearly without too much technical language.

Keep learning new skills that will be valuable in an AI-powered world. These aren't just technical skills – they include critical thinking, creativity, and the ability to adapt to new situations. These human skills become more important as AI handles more routine tasks.

Help build connections in your community around AI awareness. Share what you learn with neighbors, coworkers, and friends. When more people understand AI, communities can make better decisions about how to use it.

Moving Forward

Taking action on AI issues might seem challenging, but remember that small steps matter. Every time you make an informed choice about AI, report a problem, or help someone understand these technologies better, you're making a difference.

In our final chapter, we'll look at practical resources you can use to keep learning and stay involved in shaping how AI affects your life. We'll provide specific tools, organizations, and information sources you can turn to for help.

[Next: Part 7 - Practical Resources]

Remember: You don't need to be a technical expert to have a say in how AI is used. Your experiences and concerns matter, and there are many ways to make your voice heard.

PART 7: PRACTICAL RESOURCES

Easy-to-Use AI Tools

L et's start with tools you can use safely today. These are AI programs that can help you with everyday tasks without putting your privacy at risk.

Voice Assistants You Can Trust: Not all voice assistants are the same. For example, Apple's Siri and DuckDuckGo's assistant focus more on protecting your privacy than others. They keep most of your information on your device instead of sending it to the internet. When you set up a voice assistant, look in the privacy settings. You can usually turn off things like recording storage or personalized advertising.

Writing Help: If you need help writing emails or documents, there are safe AI writing tools you can use. Grammarly helps catch spelling and grammar mistakes, and its free version works well for most people. Microsoft Word now includes AI writing suggestions that can help make your writing clearer. Just remember to read over anything AI helps you write to make sure it says what you want.

Photo and Video Tools: Many phone cameras now use AI to help take better pictures. These tools are safe to use because they work right on your phone. For editing photos, apps like Snapseed use AI to help improve your pictures without sending them to the internet. Just be careful with apps that ask to send your photos somewhere else – they might keep and use your pictures in ways you don't want.

Where to Learn More

Finding good information about AI doesn't have to be hard. Here are trustworthy places to learn more:

Public Libraries: Your local library likely has free classes about technology and AI. Librarians can help you find books that explain AI in simple terms. Many libraries also offer free access to online learning websites like LinkedIn Learning or Coursera, where you can take AI courses at your own pace.

Government Resources: The Federal Trade Commission (FTC) website has a section called "Consumer Information" with clear explanations about AI and your rights. The National Institute of Standards and Technology (NIST) offers simple guides about AI safety and privacy.

Educational Websites:

- Common Sense Media explains AI in clear language and rates AI tools for safety
- Khan Academy offers free lessons about AI and technology
- Consumer Reports regularly publishes easy-to-understand articles about AI products and privacy

Help and Support Groups

You're not alone in trying to understand and deal with AI. There are groups that can help:

Local Tech Groups: Many communities have technology meetup groups where people help each other learn about new tools. Your local library or community center can help you find these groups.

Online Communities: Facebook groups like "AI Learning for Beginners" and "Tech Support for Seniors" can be helpful places to ask questions and share experiences. Just remember not to share personal information in these groups.

Consumer Protection Organizations: Organizations like Consumer Reports and the Electronic Frontier Foundation work to protect people's rights with technology. They often have helpful newsletters and guides you can use.

Legal Rights and AI

Understanding your legal rights with AI doesn't require a law degree. Here are the basics you need to know:

Your Data Rights:

- You have the right to know what information companies collect about you
- You can ask companies to show you your data
- You can request that companies delete your information
- You can opt out of many types of data collection

When Things Go Wrong: If you have problems with AI systems, you can:

- File complaints with the Federal Trade Commission
- Contact your state's consumer protection office
- Report problems to the Better Business Bureau
- Seek help from consumer protection lawyers who offer free consultations

Emergency Contacts and Resources

Keep these contacts handy in case you have problems with AI systems:

For Identity Theft:

- Identity Theft Resource Center: 1-888-400-5530 (free help)
- Federal Trade Commission ID Theft Hotline: 1-877-438-4338

For Online Scams:

- FBI's Internet Crime Complaint Center (IC3) website
- Local police non-emergency number (save this in your phone)

For Privacy Violations:

- Your state's attorney general's office
- Electronic Privacy Information Center (EPIC)

Important Updates to Know About

AI technology changes quickly. Here's how to stay informed without getting overwhelmed:

Easy-to-Read News Sources:

- Consumer Reports' technology section
- NPR's technology news

- USA Today's tech section These sources explain AI news in simple terms.

Government Updates: Sign up for FTC consumer alerts to get important updates about AI scams and safety issues. They send simple, clear emails when there's something you need to know.

Company Announcements: When companies like Google, Apple, or Microsoft make important changes to their AI tools, they usually explain these changes in their apps or on their websites. Look for messages that say "Important Update" or "Privacy Notice."

Using This Book Going Forward

Keep this book as a reference guide. When you're unsure about something related to AI:

1. Look up the topic in the relevant chapter
2. Check the resources listed here for updated information
3. Follow the step-by-step advice
4. Reach out to the help sources mentioned if you need more support

Remember: Technology will keep changing, but the basic principles of protecting yourself and using AI wisely will stay the same. Focus on understanding these basics, and you'll be better prepared for whatever changes come next.

Final Thoughts

You don't have to become an AI expert to use these technologies safely and effectively. Keep this resource guide handy, stay informed through trusted sources, and don't hesitate to ask for help when you need it. The resources listed here are designed to support you as AI becomes more common in our daily lives.

Remember that you have the right to understand and control how AI affects your life. Use these resources to help you make informed choices and protect yourself and your family as technology continues to evolve.

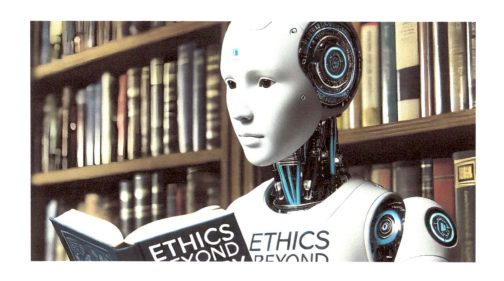

QUICK REFERENCE GUIDE: ESSENTIAL AI INFORMATION AND RESOURCES

Identity Theft:
- Identity Theft Resource Center: 1-888-400-5530
- FTC Identity Theft Hotline: 1-877-438-4338

Scams and Fraud:
- FTC Consumer Hotline: 1-877-382-4357
- FBI Internet Crime Center: www.ic3.gov

Privacy Help:
- Electronic Privacy Center: www.epic.org
- FTC Consumer Response: 1-877-FTC-HELP

Safety Checklist for AI Tools

Before using any new AI tool, ask:

1. What personal information does it want?

2. Where will my information be stored?
3. Can I delete my information later?
4. Is there a privacy policy I can read?
5. Do I really need to share this information?

Quick Privacy Settings Guide

Phone Settings:

- Location Services: Settings → Privacy → Location Services
- App Permissions: Settings → Privacy → Check each category
- Microphone Access: Settings → Privacy → Microphone

Social Media Basic Privacy:

- Facebook: Settings → Privacy → Limit Past Posts
- Instagram: Settings → Privacy → Account Privacy → Private Account
- Twitter/X: Settings → Privacy and Safety → Protected Tweets

Voice Assistants:

- Amazon Alexa: Alexa app → Settings → Privacy
- Google Assistant: Google Home app → Settings → Privacy
- Siri: Settings → Siri & Search → Siri History

Warning Signs of AI Scams

Watch out if:

- Someone calls using a family member's voice asking for money
- An AI-generated message creates urgency about your accounts
- A too-good-to-be-true offer requires immediate action

- Someone asks you to pay by gift cards or wire transfer
- An official-looking email asks for personal information

Safe AI Tools for Daily Use

Writing Help:
- Grammarly (free version)
- Microsoft Editor
- Google Docs smart compose

Photo Tools:
- Your phone's built-in AI camera features
- Snapseed
- Google Photos editing tools

Voice Assistants:
- Siri (Apple)
- DuckDuckGo assistant
- Firefox voice search

Your Basic AI Rights

You have the right to:
1. Know when AI is making decisions about you
2. Challenge automated decisions
3. Access your personal data
4. Request deletion of your data
5. Opt out of AI surveillance
6. Receive clear explanations

Monthly Security Check-Up

Do these once a month:
1. Update all passwords
2. Check privacy settings on social media
3. Review app permissions
4. Delete unused apps
5. Clear voice assistant history
6. Check for software updates

Trusted Information Sources

News and Updates:
- Consumer Reports (www.consumerreports.org)
- NPR Technology News (www.npr.org/sections/technology)
- FTC Consumer Alerts (www.ftc.gov/alerts)

Learning Resources:
- Local library technology programs
- Khan Academy (www.khanacademy.org)

- Common Sense Media (www.commonsensemedia.org)

Key Terms to Know

AI Types:

- Narrow AI: Does one specific task
- AGI: Could think like humans
- ASI: Smarter than humans

Common Terms:

- Algorithm: Steps a computer follows
- Machine Learning: How AI improves
- Neural Network: AI brain structure
- Data Mining: Finding patterns in information

Protection Steps for Common Situations

If Your Identity Is Stolen:

1. Call Identity Theft Hotline
2. Place a fraud alert with credit bureaus
3. File a police report
4. Contact your banks
5. Document everything

If You Spot a Scam:

1. Stop all contact
2. Report to FTC
3. Alert your bank
4. Warn family members
5. Keep all evidence

If Your Data Is Breached:

1. Change all passwords
2. Enable two-factor authentication

3. Monitor credit reports
4. Alert financial institutions
5. File complaints with relevant agencies

When to Seek Help

Get expert help if:
- You've lost money to a scam
- Your identity has been stolen
- AI makes unfair decisions about you
- You can't access your accounts
- You're being harassed online

Important Documents to Keep

Keep copies of:
1. Identity theft reports
2. Scam-related communications
3. Complaint submissions
4. Company responses
5. Credit reports

Store these securely and note the dates of all incidents and responses.

[Note: Update this guide every six months as contact information and resources may change.]

EXTRA HELP: ADDITIONAL RESOURCES AND SUPPORT

Questions to Ask Companies

W hen dealing with companies that use AI, it helps to know what to ask. Here are simple questions that can get you important answers:

About Your Data: "What exactly do you collect about me?" "Where do you store my information?" "Who can see my data?" "How long do you keep my information?" "Can I get a copy of my data?" "How do I delete my information?"

About AI Decisions: "Is AI being used to make decisions about me?" "How does your AI make decisions?" "What happens if the AI makes a mistake?" "Can a human review AI decisions?" "How can I appeal if I disagree?"

About Privacy: "How do you protect my personal information?" "Do you share my data with other companies?" "Can I opt out of data collection?" "What happens to my data if I close my account?"

Sample Letters and Forms

Here are templates you can use for common situations. Just fill in the blanks with your information:

Data Access Request

Date: [Today's Date]
To: [Company Name]
[Company Address]
Dear Sir/Madam,
I am writing to request a copy of all personal data you hold about me, as allowed
by privacy laws. My details are:
Name: [Your Name]
Email: [Your Email]
Account Number (if applicable): [Your Account Number]
Please send me:
1. All personal information you have about me
2. Where you got this information
3. Who you share it with
4. How long you keep it
Please respond within 30 days, as required by law.
Thank you for your help.
Sincerely,
[Your Name]
[Your Address]
[Your Phone Number]

AI Decision Appeal

Date: [Today's Date]
To: [Company Name]
[Company Address]
Dear Sir/Madam,
I am writing to appeal an automated decision made about my account/

application. The details are:
Decision Date: [Date]
Reference Number: [Number if you have one]
Type of Decision: [What was decided]
I believe this decision was incorrect because:
[Explain your reasons simply]
I request:
1. A human review of this decision
2. An explanation of how the decision was made
3. What I can do to change this outcome
Please respond within 14 days.
Thank you for your attention to this matter.
Sincerely,
[Your Name]
[Your Contact Information]

Where to File Complaints

Keep this list of places where you can report problems:

For Privacy Issues:

- Your state's Attorney General's office
- Federal Trade Commission (FTC) website
- Consumer Financial Protection Bureau
- Better Business Bureau

For Online Safety:

- FBI's Internet Crime Complaint Center (IC3)
- Federal Communications Commission
- Your local police department
- National Cyber Security Alliance

For Consumer Protection:

- State consumer protection office
- Federal Trade Commission

- Consumer Financial Protection Bureau
- Your local consumer affairs office

Local Resources Guide

Here's how to find help in your area:

Libraries:

- Ask about free computer classes
- Look for tech help sessions
- Join digital literacy programs
- Use free internet access

Community Centers:

- Check for technology workshops
- Find computer access programs
- Join senior tech training
- Attend safety seminars

Senior Centers:

- Look for tech training classes
- Join phone and tablet workshops
- Find scam prevention programs
- Get one-on-one tech help

Schools and Colleges:

- Adult education programs
- Community tech workshops
- Free online learning access
- Student volunteer tech help

Timeline: When to Do What

Daily:

- Check account notifications
- Review unusual emails or messages
- Update apps when prompted
- Back up important information

Weekly:

- Check account activity
- Clear browser history
- Update passwords if needed
- Review app permissions

Monthly:

- Check credit card statements
- Update security software
- Review privacy settings
- Delete unused apps

Yearly:

- Get free credit reports
- Review all online accounts
- Update emergency contacts
- Check privacy policies

Common Problems and Solutions

Problem: **"I think my identity was stolen."** Solution:

1. Call Identity Theft Hotline: 1-888-400-5530
2. Place a fraud alert with credit bureaus
3. File a police report
4. Contact your banks
5. Keep records of everything

Problem: **"An AI system made a wrong decision about me."** Solution:

1. Request an explanation in writing
2. Ask for a human review
3. Gather supporting documents
4. File a formal appeal
5. Contact consumer protection if needed

Problem: **"I keep getting scam calls and messages."** Solution:

1. Register for Do Not Call list
2. Report numbers to FTC
3. Block suspicious numbers
4. Update privacy settings
5. Install call blocking apps

Learning Resources by Topic

Privacy Protection:

- Common Sense Privacy Program
- FTC Privacy Guides
- Library Privacy Workshops
- AARP Identity Protection Guide

Scam Prevention:

- FTC Scam Alerts
- AARP Fraud Watch
- Local Police Updates
- Consumer Reports Guides

AI Understanding:

- Khan Academy Tech Courses
- Library Technology Programs
- Senior Planet Classes
- PBS Digital Learning

Remember: Keep this Extra Help section with your Quick Reference Guide. Together, they give you tools to handle most AI-related situations you might face.

[Note: Contact information and resources should be verified and updated regularly as they may change.]

BIBLIOGRAPHY AND FURTHER READING

Basic AI Understanding

Broussard, Meredith. "Artificial Unintelligence: How Computers Misunderstand the World." MIT Press, 2023.

- A clear explanation of AI's capabilities and limitations

Howard, Jeremy and Sylvain Gugger. "Deep Learning for Coders with Fastai and PyTorch." O'Reilly Media, 2023.

- Practical examples of how AI systems work

Mitchell, Melanie. "Artificial Intelligence: A Guide for Thinking Humans." Pelican Books, 2022.

- Straightforward introduction to AI concepts

AI in Daily Life

Christian, Brian and Tom Griffiths. "Algorithms to Live By." Henry Holt and Co., 2022.

- How computer thinking affects everyday decisions

O'Neil, Cathy. "Weapons of Math Destruction." Crown, 2023.

- How AI affects ordinary people's lives

Webb, Amy. "The Big Nine: How the Tech Titans and Their Thinking Machines Could Warp Humanity." PublicAffairs, 2023.

- Clear explanation of major tech companies and AI

Privacy and Security

Schneier, Bruce. "Data and Goliath." W.W. Norton & Company, 2023.

- Easy-to-understand guide to digital privacy

Choi, Hannah. "Privacy is Power." Bantam Press, 2023.

- Practical privacy protection strategies

Rothman, Lily. "The Right to Privacy in the Digital Age." Brookings Institution Press, 2023.

- Understanding privacy rights with technology

AI Safety and Ethics

Russell, Stuart. "Human Compatible." Viking, 2023.

- Making AI systems work better for people

Christian, Brian. "The Alignment Problem." W.W. Norton & Company, 2023.

- How to keep AI working in human interests

Wagoner, John "Ten Commandments for an AI." Skyrocket Ranch Press, 2024.

- What AI means for humanity's future

Tegmark, Max. "Life 3.0: Being Human in the Age of Artificial Intelligence." Knopf, 2023.

- What AI means for humanity's future

Consumer Protection

Warren, Elizabeth. "The Fight Against Big Tech." Metropolitan Books, 2023.

- Standing up to large technology companies

Pasquale, Frank. "New Laws of Robotics." Harvard University Press, 2023.

- Rules for controlling AI systems

Official Reports and Guidelines

National Security Commission on Artificial Intelligence. "Final Report." U.S. Government Publishing Office, 2023.

- Official U.S. government views on AI

European Union. "Ethics Guidelines for Trustworthy AI." European Commission, 2023.

- European standards for AI development

Helpful Websites and Online Resources

Common Sense Media www.commonsensemedia.org

- Clear explanations of technology issues

Electronic Frontier Foundation www.eff.org

· Digital rights and privacy information

Federal Trade Commission Consumer Information
www.consumer.ftc.gov

· Official consumer protection guidance

Government Documents

Federal Trade Commission. "Protecting Consumer Privacy in an Era of Rapid Change." 2023.

- Official privacy protection guidelines

National Institute of Standards and Technology. "AI Risk Management Framework." 2023.

- Understanding AI safety standards

Magazine and News Sources

Consumer Reports Technology Section
- Regular updates on AI and privacy

Scientific American (Digital Life Section)
- Clear explanations of new technology

Wired Magazine
- Current technology news and analysis

Research Organizations

Pew Research Center Reports on Technology and Society

- Public opinion and technology trends

AI Now Institute Reports

- How AI affects ordinary people

Data & Society Research Reports

- Social impact of technology

Note to Readers

This bibliography lists books and resources that explain AI in clear language. Many are available at public libraries or have free online versions. Ask your librarian for help finding these materials.

The publishing dates shown are for the most recent editions at the time of writing. Newer versions may be available. Check your library or bookstore for the latest editions.